Original title:
Reflections on Relational Resonance

Copyright © 2024 Swan Charm
All rights reserved.

Author: Paula Raudsepp
ISBN HARDBACK: 978-9916-86-596-5
ISBN PAPERBACK: 978-9916-86-597-2
ISBN EBOOK: 978-9916-86-598-9

The Pulse of Partnership

Two hearts beat close, a steady drum,
With every rhythm, they become one.
In laughter shared, and trials faced,
Together they move, no time to waste.

Echoes of dreams dance in the air,
United voices, a tender prayer.
Through storms they stand, unyielding strong,
In this embrace, where they belong.

The Warmth of Shared Spaces

In cozy corners, secrets unfold,
Stories linger, warm and bold.
The clinking cups, a gentle sound,
In shared moments, joy is found.

Candles flicker, casting soft light,
Two souls intertwine, a cozy sight.
In every glance, a world anew,
Creating memories, just me and you.

Aligning Stars

Beneath the sky, we chart our course,
In cosmic dance, we find our source.
Each twinkling light, a guiding wish,
In this vast realm, we find our bliss.

Fates entwined in the midnight glow,
Every heartbeat, a secret we show.
With whispered dreams, the universe vast,
We chase the wonders, our shadows cast.

Sunsets in Synchrony

As day departs, a canvas unfolds,
With hues of pink, and tales of old.
Two silhouettes, hand in hand,
Painting memories on the sand.

In twilight's embrace, time seems to pause,
A shared heartbeat, a whispered cause.
With every sunset, a promise stays,
In the beauty of life, forever ablaze.

Gradients of Love

In shades of dawn, our hearts align,
Whispers of warmth, like aged red wine.
Each color speaks, a story unfolds,
In gradients deep, our love behold.

Through twilight hues, we dance and play,
In soft pastels, we find our way.
With every stroke, the canvas bright,
Our love blooms boldly, a beacon of light.

Stories Woven Together

Threads of laughter, moments we share,
Tales of joy, and times of care.
In quiet corners, we build a dream,
Stories woven, like a gentle stream.

Pages turn, with every embrace,
Chapters written, in time and space.
Through joy and sorrow, hand in hand,
Together we stand, a promised land.

Constellations of Companionship

Underneath the vast, starlit skies,
Stars form shapes, where friendship lies.
Connected hearts, like constellations bright,
Guiding each other through darkest night.

In cosmic dances, our paths align,
Celestial bonds, endless and fine.
With every heartbeat, a spark ignites,
In the universe of shared delights.

Ebb and Flow of Togetherness

Like tides that rise, then gently recede,
Our love flows freely, fulfilling the need.
In each wave's push, and tender pull,
Together we thrive, both wise and full.

Through storms that gather, and calm that stays,
We navigate life in beautiful ways.
In every ebb, new shores we find,
In the flow of moments, our hearts combined.

The Pulse of Affection

In the quiet whispers of the night,
Hearts beat in rhythm, pure delight.
Soft touches linger, warmth enfolds,
A tapestry of love, forever holds.

Glimmers of hope in each shared gaze,
We find our way through life's winding maze.
With every laugh, a bond does grow,
The pulse of affection, a gentle flow.

Fragments of Us

Pieces scattered, yet they shine bright,
In shadows and light, we find our fight.
Together we mold, reform and reshape,
A mosaic of memories, our hearts escape.

Through storms we weather, hand in hand,
Building our dreams on shifting sand.
With every fragment, a story unfolds,
In the fabric of us, love's truth beholds.

Seasonal Shifts in Unity

Spring blooms forth with colors so bold,
In unity's arms, we find warmth to hold.
Summer's embrace, bright days align,
In laughter and joy, our spirits entwine.

Autumn leaves dance, painting the ground,
In changes we find the beauty profound.
Winter's chill brings us close, side by side,
Through seasonal shifts, love is our guide.

Chorus of Kindred Spirits

In the symphony of souls we sing,
A chorus of hopes that love will bring.
With harmonies sweet, our hearts combine,
In melodies woven, our lives align.

Each note a memory, every beat a chance,
In the dance of affection, we find our balance.
Together we rise, together we fall,
In this chorus of kindred spirits, we stand tall.

Seasons of Togetherness

In spring we bloom, our laughter sings,
With blossoms bright, our love takes wing.
Summer's warmth wraps us in light,
We dance beneath the stars, so bright.

Autumn whispers, leaves of gold,
In every hue, our stories told.
Winter's chill brings fireside grace,
In cozy corners, we find our place.

Being Seen, Being Heard

In the silence, I find your gaze,
A mirror reflecting, in myriad ways.
Your voice a melody, soft and true,
In every word, I feel the clue.

We carve our thoughts in the open air,
Shattering doubts, laying our hearts bare.
With every listen, a spark ignites,
Together we rise, scaling new heights.

Cadence of Companionship

In rhythm we walk, side by side,
With laughter and tears, our paths collide.
Every heartbeat a gentle tune,
Under the watch of a friendly moon.

We share our dreams like whispers light,
Building foundations with every night.
In shadows cast, our friendship's glow,
A dance of souls, forever flow.

Footsteps in the Fog

In the haze, we tread so slow,
Each step a mystery, where to go?
Your hand in mine, a guiding thread,
Through the unknown, unspoken dread.

The world may blur, but we stay near,
In whispered echoes, our path is clear.
Though visions fade, our spirits rise,
Together we seek, beyond the skies.

Intersections of Life

We meet at crossroads, where paths align,
Fleeting glances, stories intertwine.
In the dance of fate, we find our place,
Moments linger, leaving a trace.

In laughter's echo, in silence profound,
Shared experiences, love's subtle sound.
Life's tapestry woven, colors so bright,
Together we shine, a beautiful sight.

Through trials faced, and joy embraced,
In every heartbeat, our bond's interlaced.
With every choice, we shape our way,
Navigating dreams, come what may.

Seasons change, as do our schemes,
In each intersection, we chase our dreams.
Through summer's light or winter's chill,
Our spirits soar, we find the thrill.

In the end, we stand hand in hand,
At the junction of life, we understand.
These intersections, a sacred space,
A journey together, full of grace.

Harmonizing Hearts

Two melodies blend in perfect tune,
Underneath the sun, or beneath the moon.
Each note a promise, sweet and strong,
In the heart's orchestra, we belong.

With whispers soft, our spirits rise,
In a symphony written across the skies.
In the rhythm of life, we find our way,
Dancing through night, and greeting day.

In harmony forged, we face the storm,
Creating a warmth that keeps us warm.
With every challenge, we find our beat,
In the cadence of love, our hearts repeat.

Through whispers gentle, and laughter's cheer,
Our song grows louder, year after year.
Together we sing, through thick and thin,
In the music of life, we both win.

Each heartbeat's echo, a note divine,
Crafting our story, the stars align.
In this harmony, forever we'll stay,
Two hearts united, come what may.

Uncharted Territories of Togetherness

Through valleys deep, we chart the unknown,
With hearts as compass, in love we've grown.
Together we wander, hand in hand,
In the uncharted, we understand.

Across vast oceans, we set our sail,
Guided by dreams, we'll never fail.
In the blue horizon, adventures call,
Side by side, we'll conquer all.

In forests thick, where shadows play,
We find our light, come what may.
With every step on this endless road,
Our spirits lifted, we share the load.

Mountains high, and caverns low,
In unison, we watch the glow.
With every moment, our bond deepens,
In these territories, love's essence indents.

Through laughter's peaks and sorrow's bends,
In this journey, our love transcends.
Exploring together, wild and free,
In uncharted lands, it's you and me.

Echoes of Connection

In quiet whispers, our hearts collide,
Through shared glances, we cannot hide.
Echoes of laughter, a cherished sound,
In every moment, our love is found.

Through tangled paths and winding roads,
We carry each other, lightening loads.
In the depths of silence, we still speak,
In every breath, our spirits peek.

As time flows on, and seasons change,
Our bond grows deeper, never strange.
In echoes of dreams, we find our way,
Together we shine, day by day.

In the tapestry of life, threads entwine,
In every heartbeat, your soul meets mine.
Through trials and triumphs, we remain,
In this echo of love, joy and pain.

With open hearts, we'll journey forth,
In the echoes of life, we find our worth.
Together we'll dance, forever connected,
In the song of existence, beautifully reflected.

Light in Each Other's Shadows

In twilight's hush, we find our way,
With whispered dreams that softly sway.
Your presence, like a guiding star,
Illuminates the paths we are.

Together, we dance in silent grace,
Each heartbeat slips into its place.
In every shadow, light we trace,
A bond that time cannot erase.

Hands entwined, we brave the night,
In every fear, there's love's invite.
Through every doubt, we hold on tight,
For in the dark, we share our light.

With you, the world feels less unknown,
In tender moments, we've both grown.
The strength we find, our hearts have shown,
In each other's shadows, we've found home.

So let the stars above us gleam,
In twilight's glow, we chase our dream.
Together, we weave life's grand theme,
Bound by the love that makes us beam.

Symphony of Familiarity

In every laugh, a chord we play,
A melody that lights our way.
With notes of joy, our hearts align,
Creating bonds that intertwine.

The rhythm found in daily sights,
Soft whispers shared under moonlight.
Together, we hum a gentle tune,
In the silence, our hearts commune.

Each memory, a vibrant note,
With every word, emotions float.
In the symphony that we create,
Familiarity becomes our fate.

The harmony of souls in sync,
In every glance, we dare not blink.
Through stormy days, our song will rise,
A testament that never dies.

Together, we sway to the beat,
In laughter and love, we feel complete.
In our hearts, this song we greet,
A symphony where two souls meet.

Patterns of Belonging

In woven threads, our stories blend,
A tapestry that has no end.
Each stitch a moment, bright and true,
In patterns formed by me and you.

From whispered secrets to shared delight,
We sketch our dreams in colors bright.
The fabric rich with love and care,
In every tear, our souls laid bare.

The circles drawn that pull us near,
In every laugh, we conquer fear.
Within this space, we craft and mold,
A legacy that will unfold.

So let the patterns intertwine,
In every heartbeat, ties that bind.
Together we create and share,
A world that blossoms from our care.

In every moment, let it show,
The beauty in what we both know.
In every pattern, love will grow,
A sense of belonging in the flow.

The Art of Holding Space

In quiet moments, I am near,
A gentle presence, calm and clear.
With open arms, I hold your heart,
In trust and love, we'll never part.

Each spoken word, a thread we weave,
In the silence, we both believe.
Together, we embrace the raw,
In vulnerability, we find awe.

I see the storm that clouds your way,
In your sadness, I choose to stay.
Let burdens lift, and fears subside,
In this haven, we confide.

With patience, we find our release,
In shared stillness, we discover peace.
Through trials faced, we learn and grow,
In this safe space, all love will show.

Hold my hand; let's face the dawn,
In the light, we'll carry on.
Through all our journey, side by side,
The art of space, our hearts abide.

Resonant Silence

In quiet corners, shadows dance,
The stillness hums a soft romance.
Whispers curl like smoke in air,
Lost in thoughts, I linger there.

A heartbeat's echo, time stands still,
Echoing secrets, dreams to fulfill.
Voices fade, yet linger near,
Resonant silence, calm and clear.

Beneath the stars, the world unwinds,
In twilight hours, peace entwines.
Memories float like leaves in fall,
In the hush, I hear your call.

Reflective pools of dark and light,
Hold stories wrapped in twinkling night.
With each breath, old worries cease,
In resonant silence, I find peace.

The gentle breeze begins to play,
Softening the edges of the day.
It cradles whispers, sweet and kind,
In every pause, solace we find.

Sonatas of Affection

In twilight's glow, your laughter sings,
Soft echoes dance on gentle wings.
A melody woven, hearts embrace,
In sonatas of affection, time finds grace.

Through whispered notes, our spirits soar,
In every rhythm, forevermore.
Cadences build with tender flair,
Every glance whispers, 'I am there.'

Like raindrops falling on thirsty ground,
Love's harmony in every sound.
Chords entwined in the evening light,
A symphony born from shared delight.

With every heartbeat, the story grows,
In laughter's flow, affection glows.
Within the silence, music plays,
In countless moments, love conveys.

The world may shift and seasons change,
Yet our sonatas will rearrange.
In timeless verses, we shall write,
Our melody glows through day and night.

Euphony of Existence

A harmony hums in dawn's soft break,
Life's gentle rhythm, choices we make.
Each moment dances, bright and free,
In the euphony of existence, I see.

Waves crash softly on golden shores,
Whispers of nature, the spirit soars.
In colors blended, life unfolds,
A tapestry rich, a story told.

Every heartbeat sings a song,
An ode to the journey, where we belong.
In the rustling leaves, secrets thread,
Euphony echoes where dreams are fed.

Stars twinkle, thoughts intertwined,
In cosmic rhythms, we seek and find.
With open hearts, we ready the way,
To weave our tales in the light of day.

Every breath we take, a note divine,
Life's symphony plays, a precious line.
In the embrace of all that persists,
In the euphony of existence, love exists.

Lullabies of Loyalty

In the stillness of the night,
Whispers float on gentle air,
Promises born from pure delight,
A bond that timelessly we share.

Through shadows deep, we walk as one,
Hand in hand, our hearts alight,
In the laughter, and the fun,
Together, we embrace the night.

When storms arise, like thunder's roar,
We stand steadfast, a shielded wall,
Through every struggle, we explore,
Unyielding, we shall never fall.

In quiet moments, loyalty sings,
A song of trust that brightly glows,
In this heart, love gently clings,
As the river of friendship flows.

With every step, we find our way,
A journey etched in love's design,
In lullabies, come what may,
Our souls entwined, forever shine.

The Tapestry of Trust

With threads of gold and hues so bright,
We weave a tale that never frays,
In every stitch, a spark of light,
In the fabric of our days.

Through trials faced, our hands entwined,
In every challenge, we find grace,
Our hearts, like stars, forever aligned,
In trust, we forge a sacred space.

In whispered dreams, our hopes are strong,
A melody of faith we sing,
Together, we belong,
In unity, our spirits spring.

Each journey taken, side by side,
With every step, our bond is sealed,
In love's embrace, we firmly bide,
A tapestry of trust revealed.

With colors bright and patterns bold,
Our lives entwined, a story spun,
In every moment, warmth unfolds,
In this great tapestry, we're one.

Empathy's Embrace

In quiet corners, hearts convey,
The warmth of understanding's glow,
In every word, a gentle sway,
   Empathy helps us grow.

With open arms, we share our pain,
Droplets of sorrow, drops of joy,
Through every storm, through every rain,
   Connection is our greatest ploy.

In laughter and in tears, we find,
A bridge that links both soul and mind,
In every glance, compassion binds,
   In this embrace, love is defined.

With every story shared, we heal,
In empathy's warm, tender grasp,
A silent promise we reveal,
   In kindness, we forever clasp.

As lives entwine and pathways cross,
With every heartache that we view,
In empathy, we gain, not loss,
A bond of love that feels so true.

Shared Horizons

Beneath the vast and starlit sky,
We chase the dreams both near and far,
In every laugh, a joyful sigh,
Together, we are who we are.

On shared horizons, our paths align,
With every sunrise, hope takes flight,
As hands connect, our hearts combine,
In unity, we find our light.

Through valleys low and mountains high,
We share our stories, deep and wide,
With every breath, a solemn cry,
In trust, we walk with hearts open wide.

With every challenge that we meet,
We stand together, side by side,
In every victory, bittersweet,
We learn to cherish, love, and guide.

In perfect harmony, dreams arise,
With every step, our spirits soar,
On these shared horizons, love lies,
Together forever, we explore.

Waves of Intimacy

In the hush of twilight's glow,
Whispers ride the silent flow.
Hearts in rhythm, soft and deep,
Tides of trust where secrets keep.

Gentle touches brush like foam,
Every glance feels like a home.
With each wave, the distance fades,
In this sea, our love cascades.

Echoes dance upon the shore,
Promises in every roar.
Hand in hand, we wander free,
Entwined in this melody.

Stars emerge, our night unfolds,
In their light, our story molds.
Every heartbeat, every sigh,
Like the tides, we rise and fly.

In the deep, where shadows play,
Lies a truth we can't betray.
Waves of warmth, the moon's own kiss,
In this ocean, we find bliss.

The Language of Silence

In the quiet, thoughts collide,
Echoes linger, hearts confide.
A glance shared, our secrets speak,
In the stillness, we are unique.

Words unspoken, soft and light,
Fleeting shadows dance at night.
In every pause, in every breath,
Lies the strength defying death.

Silent dreams weave tales untold,
In the dark, our truths unfold.
Hands entwined without a sound,
In this space, our souls are found.

The weight of love weighs heavy here,
In the absence, we draw near.
Brevity in every glance,
In silence, we find our chance.

With spoken breaths, we bridge the gap,
In that hush, we lay the map.
Together, we create our song,
In silence, we both belong.

Intertwined Lives

Two paths merge beneath the stars,
In the night, we heal our scars.
With every step, our shadows sway,
In this dance, we find our way.

Branches twist, roots dig deep,
In this grove, our souls we keep.
A gentle touch, a knowing glance,
In this garden, we take our chance.

Time unravels, moments blend,
With every turn, our hearts transcend.
Laughing echoes in the air,
In this union, we lay bare.

Through life's storms, we stand as one,
Intertwined, we've just begun.
Fleeting days, yet we remain,
Bonded in joy and in pain.

Nature's weave, a tapestry,
Woven threads of you and me.
In the light of dawn's embrace,
We create our sacred space.

Resonant Souls

In a world where echoes blend,
Two souls meet, their paths transcend.
Harmonies in every sigh,
In their tones, the reasons lie.

Feeling rhythms, hearts attune,
In this dance, we find our tune.
From the depths, our voices rise,
A sweet song beneath the skies.

Silent prayers in whispered nights,
Resonating, bringing light.
With every note, our spirits soar,
In this music, we find more.

Hands held tight, we chase the dream,
Together, let our passions stream.
In the laughter, in the tears,
Resonance conquers all our fears.

In this symphony of grace,
Two souls strive to find their place.
As we pulse in life's embrace,
In our hearts, we leave a trace.

Harmonies in Heartbeats

In the quiet of the night,
Two hearts begin to sing,
With every gentle thrum,
Love becomes the spring.

Melodies intertwine,
Like soft whispers low,
Each beat a promise kept,
In warmth's eternal glow.

Stars above us twinkle,
As shadows sway and sway,
In the rhythm of our lives,
Together we will stay.

The world around us fades,
In symphonies of two,
With every breath we take,
Our dreams come shining through.

So listen to the song,
That echoes deep inside,
In the harmonies we share,
Our hearts forever tied.

The Dance of Souls

In a circle of soft light,
Our spirits start to spin,
With every twirl we take,
New journeys can begin.

The music calls us closer,
As laughter fills the air,
In every step we make,
There's magic everywhere.

We glide through endless moments,
Two souls in perfect time,
A dance of joy and grace,
In rhythm and in rhyme.

With every sway and fold,
The universe aligns,
Your hand within my reach,
Our heartbeat intertwines.

So let the night unfold,
As stars above us glow,
In the dance of our souls,
It's love that we bestow.

Threads of Togetherness

Woven in the fabric bright,
Are stories yet to tell,
Each thread of you and me,
In harmony we dwell.

Through laughter and through tears,
Our tapestry takes shape,
With colors bold and soft,
In memories we drape.

A stitch of shared moments,
A knot of love secure,
In every twist and turn,
Together we endure.

The fabric of our lives,
So rich with love and care,
With threads that bind us close,
Through every hope we share.

So cherish every weave,
In patterns sweetly spun,
For in these threads we find,
Our hearts are truly one.

Resonating Waves of Emotion

Waves crashing on the shore,
Echo deep within me,
Each surge, a feeling strong,
Like wild, untamed sea.

With every rise and fall,
The tides of love prevail,
In currents of devotion,
We navigate love's trail.

The echoes of our laughter,
Resonate like the breeze,
In quiet reflection,
Our souls find sweet release.

So ride the waves with me,
Through calm and storms we face,
In the ocean of our dreams,
We'll find our sacred place.

Together we will dance,
Upon the shores of time,
In resonating waves,
Our love remains sublime.

Echoes of Connection

In the stillness, whispers call,
Threads of voices, weaving all.
Connections bloom, soft and bright,
In the shadows, love takes flight.

Moments linger, memories flow,
Hearts entwined, they ebb and glow.
Silent vows, in twilight's grace,
Together they find their place.

Through the laughter, pain we share,
In the silence, knowing stares.
Every heartbeat, soft refrain,
Echoes of joy and of pain.

Time may shift, yet bonds remain,
In the distance, voices reign.
Each connection, a sacred thread,
In the fabric of love, we're led.

In every glance, a world ignites,
In the dark, shared guiding lights.
Echoes of connection, pure and true,
A tapestry woven, me and you.

The Heart's Harmonious Dance

In the quiet, hearts align,
Every pulse, a gentle sign.
Fingers brush, like notes they play,
In sweet rhythm, night and day.

Whispers linger in the air,
In this moment, souls prepare.
With each step, a story spun,
The dance of two has just begun.

Melodies rise, they intertwine,
Every glance, a spark divine.
In perfect sync, they move as one,
A radiant glow, a rising sun.

Through the music, they are free,
In this moment, just to be.
The heart's dance, a cherished trance,
In silent joy, they take their chance.

Time surrenders, lost in bliss,
In every turn, a gentle kiss.
The heart's harmonious dance unfolds,
A tale of love that never grows old.

Whispers in the Air

In the twilight, secrets weave,
Soft and gentle, they believe.
Echoes float on midnight's breeze,
Whispers shared with simple ease.

Every sigh, a tale untold,
In the silence, hearts unfold.
Through the shadows, stories glide,
In the spaces, love abides.

Laughter mingles, light and free,
In the distance, harmony.
Words unspoken, deeply felt,
In the air, emotions melt.

With the dawn, new hopes arise,
In the sunrise, truths surprise.
Whispers dancing on the light,
In the morning, spirits bright.

In each heartbeat, truth revealed,
All the dreams that love has sealed.
Whispers in the air, so rare,
A tapestry of love we share.

Chords of Togetherness

In the strum of life, we find,
Chords of joy, sweetly entwined.
Melodies rise, soft and clear,
In togetherness, we draw near.

Hands in harmony, hearts embrace,
In this music, we find grace.
Every note, a bond we weave,
In this symphony, we believe.

Through the laughter, through the tears,
In every echo, calm our fears.
Chords of togetherness resound,
In this rhythm, love is found.

As we dance through shifting skies,
In every heartbeat, love complies.
The universe, in tune, aligns,
Chords of life, our hearts combine.

In the quiet, in the play,
Chords unite in bright array.
Together we rise, hand in hand,
In harmony, forever stand.

Tapestry of Trust

In the weave of our hearts, a promise stands,
Each thread a whisper, binding our hands.
Through storms that may come, we hold on tight,
In the tapestry of trust, we find our light.

With colors so vibrant, the hues intertwine,
Every joy and sorrow, a blessing divine.
Together we rise, with courage, we thread,
In the fabric of life, no words left unsaid.

In moments of doubt, we weave on with care,
A journey of faith, no burden to bear.
With every heartbeat, we stitch the design,
In this tapestry of trust, our lives align.

The Canvas of Kinship

On the canvas of kinship, our stories unfold,
Brush strokes of laughter, in colors so bold.
Each moment a masterpiece, crafted in time,
In the gallery of love, our hearts intertwine.

With shadows and light, we paint every scene,
Together through struggles, our spirits serene.
United in purpose, we draw from within,
In the canvas of kinship, we always begin.

With each gentle stroke, we deepen the hue,
In the bonds of our family, forever we're true.
Through trials and triumphs, our art shall remain,
A canvas of kinship, through joy and through pain.

Unraveled Threads

As threads come undone, new patterns appear,
Life's fabric unravels, revealing our fears.
Yet woven with patience, we gather the strands,
In the tapestry's heart, together we stand.

The colors may fade, but hope holds us tight,
Through darkness we journey, toward the light.
In each whispered story, a thread still remains,
Connecting our souls through joys and through pains.

With hands intertwined, we mend what has frayed,
In the loom of our lives, love never will jade.
For every unraveled, a new path we see,
In the threads of our lives, we find unity.

Heartbeats in Unison

In the silence we share, our heartbeats collide,
A rhythm of longing, two souls opened wide.
With each gentle pulse, our stories unite,
In the dance of the heart, we soar to new heights.

In moments of stillness, our spirits embrace,
Through trials and triumphs, we find our own space.
Each heartbeat a promise, in shadows and sun,
Together forever, our journeys are one.

Through laughter and tears, we echo the beat,
In this symphony sweet, we all find our seat.
With love as the conductor, we find our way through,
In heartbeats in unison, forever we're true.

Echoing Laughter

In the gentle breeze, laughter flies,
Dancing through trees, touching the skies.
A melody sweet, pure and bright,
Echoes of joy, in soft twilight.

Whispers of fun, with each shared smile,
Every moment cherished, for a while.
In waves of sound, hearts intertwine,
A symphony formed, your laugh, my sign.

Through fields we run, so light and free,
The world a stage, just you and me.
In every tickle, in every tease,
Laughter ripples, it brings us ease.

By the fireside, stories unfold,
Adventures retold, memories gold.
In the echoes, our spirits soar,
Together we shine, forevermore.

So let us embrace, this joyful ride,
With laughter as light, our faithful guide.
In the heart's deep well, joy will last,
And echo forever, binding the past.

In each other's Eyes

In each other's gaze, a story begins,
A universe blooms, where love always wins.
Silent confessions, deep and profound,
In every glance, our souls are unbound.

Windows to dreams, where hopes collide,
Reflections shining, where hearts confide.
In laughter and tears, through joy and strife,
In each other's eyes, we find our life.

Moments captured, like stars that align,
Holding the warmth of a love divine.
In every heartbeat, recognition flows,
In each other's eyes, true magic grows.

Time dances softly, yet we remain,
In the trust of looks, we'll never wane.
With dreams intertwining, like vines that climb,
In each other's eyes, we conquer time.

So gaze ever deeper, no need for disguise,
In the depths of truth, our spirit lies.
Together we'll wander, through storms and skies,
Finding forever, in each other's eyes.

Vibration of Friendship

In the rhythm of life, friends unite,
A melody shared, shining so bright.
With laughter and tears, we boldly sing,
In the vibration of friendship, hearts take wing.

Through moments of joy, through trials we face,
Together in balance, we find our place.
With every heartbeat, a bond that ties,
In the vibration of friendship, love never dies.

Supporting each other, through thick and thin,
With courage and strength, we always win.
In laughter's dance, in the warmth of goodbyes,
In the vibration of friendship, our spirit flies.

So let's raise our voices, let the world see,
The power of us, and how strong we can be.
With memories cherished, like stars in the skies,
In the vibration of friendship, our bond never lies.

Through seasons we travel, our hearts intertwined,
A beautiful journey, so thoughtfully designed.
In the melody played, where the true love lies,
In the vibration of friendship, our souls arise.

Harmonies of the Heart

In soft melodies, two souls entwined,
Creating a symphony, uniquely aligned.
With every note played, love takes its part,
In the harmonies of the heart.

Through gentle whispers, secrets we share,
In the quiet moments, showing we care.
With laughter and tears, a sweet refrain,
In the harmonies of the heart, joy remains.

As seasons shift, and time sways slow,
Together we flourish, together we grow.
In the rhythm of life, wherever we start,
In the harmonies of the heart, we'll never part.

With dreams painted bright, our canvas unfurls,
Creating memories, our precious pearls.
In every embrace, in all that we chart,
In the harmonies of the heart, love is the art.

So let's sing together, through storm and through sun,
In the dance of our lives, we both are as one.
With love as our guide, we play every part,
In the harmonies of the heart, we'll never depart.

Veins of Understanding

In quiet corners, thoughts converge,
A dance of souls in softest urge.
Words like rivers gently flow,
Through veins of knowing, deep we go.

Each whisper carries stories old,
In silken threads of hearts untold.
Embrace the silence, let it speak,
In fragile moments, wisdoms seek.

A glance exchanged, a smile shared,
In fleeting glances, love laid bare.
Within the whispers, truth we find,
Veins of understanding, intertwined.

Through tangled paths, we wander free,
With every heartbeat, unity.
An echo of what lies ahead,
The ties that bind, where faith is fed.

So let us walk, each step a chance,
In harmony's ever-present dance.
For in our hearts, connections gleam,
Veins of understanding, like a dream.

Threads Woven in Time

In fabric rich, our stories blend,
Threads woven tight, where shadows bend.
Each stitch a moment, bright and bold,
In the tapestry, tales unfold.

Time's gentle hands, they pull and weave,
Creating patterns we believe.
With every twist, a memory spins,
Chronicles of loss and wins.

Colors merge in a vibrant hue,
Reflecting all that we hold true.
Threads of laughter, tears and grace,
Intertwined in life's embrace.

As seasons change, the fabric flows,
In whispers soft, our essence glows.
Woven together, we navigate,
In this grand weave, we find our fate.

With every thread, the past ignites,
Guiding us through long, starry nights.
In unity, we come to see,
Threads woven in time, eternally.

The Poetry of Presence

In every heartbeat, life unfolds,
A silent rhythm, tales untold.
Moments linger in gentle sway,
The poetry of presence, here to stay.

With open hearts, we share the space,
Eyes that tell of time and grace.
Each glance a line, a verse alive,
In stillness deep, our spirits thrive.

Breath by breath, the world we weave,
In tender echoes, we believe.
Every heartbeat, every sigh,
Carries meaning as time slips by.

Together caught in this embrace,
We find the magic of our place.
The simplest joys, like birds that sing,
Are verses rich, to which we cling.

In presence pure, connections bloom,
Dispelling shadows, dissipating gloom.
For in each moment, love connects,
The poetry of presence, it reflects.

Rhythms of Together

In harmony we find our song,
Where every note and breath belong.
A rhythm beats in hearts aligned,
In unity, our souls combined.

With laughter shared and hands held tight,
We dance through day and into night.
In every step, a story grows,
The journey shared, a love that shows.

Through gentle winds and storms that rage,
We turn each page, we write our age.
The pulse of life, a shared delight,
In every dark, we find the light.

Together we create the mold,
Of dreams ignited, stories bold.
In rhythms found and bonds we weave,
In every heartbeat, we believe.

So let us dance, let us be free,
In every moment, you and me.
For in this rhythm, life's a treasure,
The rhythms of together, purest pleasure.

Tides of Empathy

Waves crash softly on the shore,
Whispers of hearts, longing for more.
With every ebb, with every flow,
We learn to heal, we learn to grow.

In quiet moments, we find our grace,
Holding each other in a warm embrace.
The tides may rise, the tides may fall,
Yet empathy binds us through it all.

Together we wander, side by side,
In the ocean's depths, we cannot hide.
Each story shared like the salt and sea,
Together we sail in unity.

Through storms we venture, in laughter we sing,
The currents of kindness, a beautiful thing.
With open hearts, we chart our way,
Born from the night, we'll greet the day.

Let every wave remind us to care,
The tides of empathy, strong and rare.
In every crest, and in every trough,
We rise as one; we shall not scoff.

Mirrors of the Soul

In the glass, reflections play,
Fleeting images, bright as day.
Each glance a journey, deep and wide,
Mirrors speak truths we cannot hide.

Within the gaze, we find a friend,
Silent echoes, love to send.
Through fleeting moments, hearts unveil,
The stories hidden, the dreams that sail.

We see our flaws, our radiant light,
In shadows cast, we find our sight.
A tapestry woven with every glance,
In mirrored silence, we learn to dance.

Through glassy barriers, souls entwine,
In laughter shared, we redefine.
Each shimmer a tale, a whispered note,
In the mirrors of the soul, we float.

Reflections linger, understood,
In every pulse, they leave us good.
The heart's great echo, forever bold,
In mirrors of the soul, we behold.

Threads of Understanding

Woven softly, the threads align,
In tapestry of thoughts, divine.
Each color brightens the canvas wide,
With threads of understanding, side by side.

We stitch the moments, rich and rare,
Binding hearts with love and care.
In conversation, our truths unfold,
Each fiber woven, a story told.

Through trials and laughter, we intertwine,
As threads unite, we brightly shine.
In the fabric of life, we find our place,
Through shared experiences, we embrace.

From differing paths, we learn and grow,
With open hearts, the colors flow.
In every stitch, the bond enhances,
The threads of understanding, life's dances.

Let us weave a world that's strong and warm,
Embracing differences, shelter from storm.
Together we craft, in unity stand,
With threads of understanding, hand in hand.

Sonnet of Shared Moments

In fleeting seconds, moments reside,
Echoes of laughter that time cannot hide.
Together we gather, both light and shade,
In the heart's chambers, memories made.

With every heartbeat, whispers align,
A sonnet of souls, forever entwined.
In shared silences, our spirits soar,
In the tapestry woven, we crave for more.

The sun sets gently on stories profound,
Each moment a treasure in love we have found.
In twilight's glow, our hopes ignite,
In the fabric of time, our dreams take flight.

Through seasons that change, we shall remember,
The warmth of connection, our souls at ember.
In every heartbeat, we celebrate,
The sonnet of shared moments, our fate.

From dusk until dawn, our hearts will sing,
Together we rise, in joy we cling.
In the symphony of life, let us play,
A sonnet of moments, come what may.

The Fabric of Us

Threads of laughter weave our days,
In patterns bright, through sun and haze.
Stitching memories, strong and true,
The fabric of us, always in view.

Embroidered dreams in every seam,
A tapestry built on a shared dream.
Woven tightly, yet free to flow,
In the warmth of love, we let it glow.

Each knot a challenge, carefully tied,
In this quilt of life, we take in stride.
Colors blend, both dark and light,
Together we shine, in day and night.

Frayed edges remind us of our flaws,
Yet strengthen the bond, without a pause.
Together we rise, we mend, we grow,
In the fabric of us, our stories glow.

Notes from Within

Whispers echo in quiet rooms,
In hidden corners, the spirit blooms.
Melodies rise from the depths of soul,
Each note a journey, each sound a whole.

Rhythms dance in the silent heart,
Creating music, a sacred art.
The pulse of dreams, like beating drums,
In every heartbeat, a song becomes.

Cacophony fades to a gentle sigh,
The truth of silence, we let fly.
Every moment a chance to sing,
In notes from within, our spirits take wing.

Chords unite in harmony's embrace,
A symphony found in every face.
The essence of life, played soft, played loud,
In the notes from within, we stand proud.

Interlaced Journeys

Paths entwined beneath the stars,
Leading us close despite the scars.
Each journey unique, yet so aligned,
In the web of life, our hearts combined.

Footsteps echo on familiar ground,
Voices intertwine with every sound.
In the shadows, light begins to show,
Together we venture, together we grow.

Through valleys low and mountains high,
The bond we share can never die.
A tapestry of travels, sharp and sweet,
In interlaced journeys, our lives complete.

Guided by stars that softly shine,
Every twist and turn a sacred sign.
With open hearts, we find a way,
In each other's warmth, we choose to stay.

The Symphony of Kinship

Each note we share creates a score,
A symphony of kinship at its core.
With harmonies rich that rise and swell,
In the heart's orchestra, we find our spell.

Strings strummed gently, love's refrain,
In every chord, joy mingles with pain.
Together, we compose a timeless song,
In the symphony of kinship, we belong.

The winds of change may sometimes blow,
Yet in our hearts, the music flows.
Through crescendos and soft retreats,
The symphony of kinship never cheats.

Drums of courage guide our way,
In rhythm with love, come what may.
A melody woven through trials and cheer,
In the symphony of kinship, we hold dear.

Candles in the Dark

In silence glows the gentle flame,
A flicker strong against the night.
Each shadow whispered, with no name,
A dance of hope, a guiding light.

They burn for dreams, both lost and found,
In corners where the fears reside.
Each melted drop, a truth unbound,
A testament of souls, our guide.

Though darkness wraps its cloak around,
The candles stand, firm and bright.
Together, strength in flames we've crowned,
Defying all that flees from light.

Softly they sway in tender breeze,
In unity, a flicker grows.
A symphony of whispered pleas,
With every spark, the courage flows.

So let them burn, these candles rare,
In every heart, a flickering glow.
For in the dark, we find our care,
And light the path for those who glow.

The Essence of Standing Together

Upon the ground, we make our stand,
With hands entwined, we share our might.
A bond unbroken, a steadfast band,
In unity, we face the fight.

With every challenge, hearts align,
Through storms that try to tear apart.
Together, we forge paths that shine,
A symphony of steadfast heart.

In whispered doubts, we find our strength,
Support, the essence of our bond.
Through every trial, we go great lengths,
For in each other, we respond.

The world may falter, but we stand tall,
Shoulder to shoulder, side by side.
In all our actions, we hear the call,
Together proud, we do abide.

So hand in hand, let's face the day,
With courage deep and voices strong.
For standing together lights the way,
And in our hearts, we all belong.

Embracing the Distance

Though miles may stretch between our souls,
Our hearts beat strong in silent time.
In every thought, a bond consoles,
A love that distances can't climb.

The stars align in distant skies,
For every moment we are apart.
A warmth that glows, it never dies,
Each heartbeat echoes in the heart.

The winds carry whispers of the past,
And dreams that weave through aching nights.
With every breath, the shadows cast,
We find our strength in hidden lights.

We hold the memories close in mind,
Like precious jewels through sunsets dim.
In our embrace, the world unwinds,
And love's sweet song will never skim.

So as the distance holds its sway,
We rise above the fear and doubt.
Together still, come what may,
In every heartbeat, we're without.

Canvas of Connection

Upon this canvas, colors blend,
With strokes of laughter, tears defined.
Each hue a story, love unbends,
From every soul, a pattern twined.

In vibrant shades, our voices rise,
A melody of hearts, enthralled.
With every glance, a deep surprise,
In tangled threads, our lives are scrawled.

The brush of fate, it paints the path,
Where moments forge our tapestry.
In every swirl, there lies our math,
A harmony in mystery.

Through every struggle, joy appears,
In scribbles that become our art.
Together, we shed laughter's tears,
And canvas turns from grief to heart.

So let us gather, colors bold,
And create a world that feels alive.
In every stroke, our truths unfold,
A canvas bright, where spirits thrive.

Intimate Dialogues

In whispered tones, the secrets sway,
Hearts open wide, no words betray.
Promises linger in soft gazes,
A quiet bond that gently raises.

Fingers entwined, we share our dreams,
Glances exchanged like silver beams.
Every silence, a voiced connection,
In this space, a sweet reflection.

Moments linger with a tender grace,
Each heartbeat feels like a warm embrace.
Veiled thoughts dance in the evening air,
In our world, there's little to compare.

Outside fades, just you and I,
Underneath our canvas sky.
Veins pulse softly with heartfelt truth,
Each note resounds, echoing youth.

So let the night cradle our souls,
With every laughter, the galaxy rolls.
In this dialogue, we both belong,
Two hearts creating their own song.

Cadences of Companionship

Side by side, we craft our tune,
The world a stage under the moon.
In laughter shared, our spirits soar,
A melody played, forever more.

Each stride syncs in perfect sway,
Time stands still, come what may.
With every dream and every cheer,
Your pulse is mine, our rhythm clear.

In shadows cast by evening's glow,
Together we face the ebb and flow.
Harmony we build with care,
In every glance, a love laid bare.

Days unfold with a gentle sound,
In this companionship, we are found.
Each touch, each sigh, a note divine,
In the song of us, our hearts entwine.

So let the cadence guide our way,
Through sunlit paths or skies of gray.
Together we'll dance, ever free,
In this symphony of you and me.

Portraits of Familiarity

In colors bright, our lives displayed,
Each stroke a memory we have made.
Familiar smiles, stories retold,
In every canvas, our hearts unfold.

Soft laughter paints the deepest hue,
In every glance, a world anew.
A tapestry woven with love's embrace,
In each thread lies our secret place.

Gentle touches, the brush of time,
A delicate dance, a silent rhyme.
Every moment, a snapshot clear,
In this gallery, you draw near.

The warmth of light through open doors,
Familiar paths we walk on shores.
Jogging memories, time stands still,
In this portrait, we feel the thrill.

Captured frames hold our sweetest dreams,
With every gaze, the heart redeems.
In familiarity, we find our art,
Two souls united, never apart.

The Essence of Togetherness

In every breath, we share a grace,
A simple touch, a warm embrace.
Two souls dancing in twilight's glow,
In each heartbeat, essence flows.

Hand in hand, we face the day,
As moments weave between our play.
Each glance a promise, soft and true,
Illuminated by skies so blue.

In laughter shared on sunlit trails,
Together we create our sails.
With every storm, we stand as one,
In togetherness, we've just begun.

The world dissolves as we draw near,
In whispers shared, we conquer fear.
Our spirits rise, a fervent flight,
In unity, we find our light.

So let the journey never cease,
In your presence, I find my peace.
In the essence of us, I forever dwell,
A tale of togetherness, timeless to tell.

The Fabric of Together

In every thread, a story we weave,
Moments shared, in hearts we believe.
Colors blend, and shadows play,
Together we rise, come what may.

Laughter echoing, soft and bright,
We find our way, in the night.
Hands intertwined, a gentle embrace,
In this tapestry, we find our place.

Through every storm, we stand tall,
Bound by love, we conquer all.
Stitches of joy, patches of pain,
In this fabric, we'll never wane.

We gather strength, side by side,
In unity, we take pride.
Threads of kindness, woven tight,
A shared journey, pure delight.

As years unfold, and seasons change,
Our fabric grows, rearranged.
Yet through it all, one thing is clear,
Together we thrive, year after year.

Verses in our Veins

Words like rivers, flowing free,
Whispers shared, just you and me.
Ink of dreams, we script our fate,
In verses penned, we celebrate.

Pulsing rhythms of love and trust,
In our laughter, the world is a must.
Pages turn with every sigh,
In the chapters, our hearts fly.

Echoes linger in quiet halls,
In the silence, our spirit calls.
Verses dance upon our skin,
In each heartbeat, we begin.

Stories stitched in cosmic light,
We rise together, day and night.
Through the verses, our souls align,
In this symphony, you are mine.

Each stanza a heartbeat, strong and true,
Written in skies, just me and you.
With every breath, we craft our tale,
In the verses, we shall prevail.

Beats of Connection

In the rhythm of hearts, we find our way,
A dance of life, come what may.
Every pulse, a story untold,
In the warmth of presence, we unfold.

Melodies shared in tranquil nights,
With every glance, the world ignites.
Beats collide in joyous refrain,
In harmony, we conquer pain.

Syncopated breaths, a gentle song,
Inviting the weary to belong.
Together we weave this sacred tune,
Under the watchful gaze of the moon.

Every laugh, a note on the wind,
In this symphony, we find the blend.
Resonating strong, with echoes deep,
In our connection, promises keep.

As time rolls on, our rhythm stays,
In every heartbeat, love displays.
The beats of connection, forever entwined,
In this dance of life, our souls aligned.

Starlit Conversations

Under a sky, where dreams align,
We share our stories, like vintage wine.
Whispers float on a gentle breeze,
In starlit conversations, hearts find ease.

Each twinkle holds a secret rare,
A cosmic bond, beyond compare.
With every word, the night expands,
As galaxies form from our hands.

In the quiet, a universe stirs,
While the night hums, and the heart purrs.
Through shadows deep, we illuminate,
In starlit conversations, we create.

Dreams unravel, like silk threads spun,
In each moment, we're softly undone.
With every sigh, the stars ignite,
A celestial canvas, pure and bright.

As the dawn whispers a gentle goodbye,
In our hearts, the constellations lie.
Starlit conversations linger on,
In the fabric of time, we are never gone.

Soundscapes of Shared Moments

Whispers of laughter fill the air,
Echoes of joy beyond compare.
In twilight's glow, our stories blend,
A melody that knows no end.

Fingers entwined in quiet grace,
Time dances softly, a warm embrace.
Each heartbeat sings, a gentle tune,
In the shadow of the silver moon.

The rustle of leaves, a soft sigh,
As memories weave, and moments fly.
With every glance, our spirits soar,
Creating symphonies we adore.

Every whisper, a note so bright,
In shared silence, we find our light.
The world fades out, and still we stay,
In the soundscape of yesterday.

Through laughter's echo, we find our way,
In a chorus of dreams, we long to play.
As twilight falls, and stars ignite,
Our hearts compose the endless night.

Tides of Together

Waves of laughter crash and play,
As time flows gently, come what may.
On shores of trust, we carve our names,
In tide pools formed by shared refrains.

The ocean whispers secrets deep,
In currents strong, our bond we keep.
Together sailing toward the sun,
Each wave a journey, just begun.

Beneath the sky, our dreams unite,
In moonlit dances, pure delight.
As tides recede, we hold what's true,
The ebb and flow of me and you.

With every rise and every fall,
We find our strength, we hear the call.
In salted air and sunset glow,
The tides remind us what we know.

As waves embrace the sandy shore,
In each moment, we ask for more.
Together, we can face the storm,
In love's embrace, we stay warm.

The Pulse of Affinity

In rhythm's beat, our hearts align,
A shared pulse flowing, pure and fine.
Through silent glances, we ignite,
A tune of love, a bond so tight.

With every laugh, we raise the bar,
In a dance of warmth, we find our star.
Unspoken truths beneath the skin,
In the pulse of life, we delve within.

Our bodies sway like trees in spring,
In the gentle breeze, our spirits sing.
Each shared heartbeat, a note so clear,
In harmony, we lose our fear.

Connections deep, like roots entwined,
In the soil of love, our hearts aligned.
Together thriving, we find our grace,
In the pulse of this sacred space.

Through life's wild rhythm, we stand strong,
In every moment, we belong.
With whispered dreams and tender sighs,
The pulse of affinity never dies.

Connections Beyond Words

In simple gestures, magic lies,
In the warmth of hands, truth defies.
A fleeting glance, a knowing smile,
In silent moments, we reconcile.

Every heartbeat speaks a tune,
In stillness found beneath the moon.
With eyes that shine, we communicate,
In love's embrace, we navigate.

Our hearts connect in the closest space,
Beyond the chatter, there's sacred grace.
Through deep embraces, we share our souls,
In wordless love, we find our roles.

Though language fails, our spirits soar,
In understanding, we ask for more.
In quiet knowing, bonds are spun,
Connections thrive when words are done.

In the silence, where love can dwell,
We find the stories we can't tell.
In meaningful looks, we create our art,
Connections beyond words, heart to heart.

Ripples of Compassion

In gentle waves we share our light,
A kindness cast, it takes its flight.
Each tender touch, a soothing balm,
Together we create a calm.

With whispered hope and open hearts,
We mend the world with loving parts.
Through laughter shared, the fears dissolve,
In compassion's arms, we all evolve.

A silent nod, a warm embrace,
In simple acts, we find our place.
Each ripple spreads, the circles grow,
In empathy, the love will flow.

From stranger's gaze to friend's wide smile,
The bond we weave goes on for miles.
In every kindness, we transform,
A rippling heart, forever warm.

Let's sow the seeds of hope today,
In every heart, let love convey.
For every soul, a gentle spark,
Ripples of light against the dark.

Unspoken Bonds

In quiet glances, secrets blend,
Two souls align, no need to tend.
A touch of hands, no words to spare,
In the silence, we're laid bare.

Through laughter shared, through tears we weep,
In every heartbeat, promises keep.
These ties we feel, no need to state,
In shadows cast, our fates await.

A knowing smile when paths align,
In the unseen, our hearts entwine.
With every moment, unvoiced grace,
In the absence, love finds its space.

Though distance parts, we still remain,
In thoughts we share, the bond won't strain.
Invisible threads that pull us near,
Unspoken bonds, forever clear.

In every dream, you linger close,
In silent prayers, I find you most.
Through winds of time, we soar above,
In every heartbeat, there's our love.

Celestial Gatherings

In twilight's glow, stars start to dance,
Each flicker holds a sacred chance.
With every wish upon the night,
The heavens hum with pure delight.

Galaxies twirl, a cosmic song,
In their embrace, we all belong.
Together drawn by fate's design,
A tapestry of love divine.

Comets blaze across the sky,
In their wake, our dreams can fly.
Each gathering whispers tales of old,
In stardust stories, hearts unfold.

When moonlight bathes the world in gold,
We gather close, our truths retold.
With every heartbeat, we ignite,
A constellation of shared light.

Through cosmic ties, we find our way,
In every night, we choose to stay.
From distant stars to heartbeats here,
Celestial love, forever clear.

The Map of Us

In every line, our stories trace,
The paths we walk, this sacred space.
Each twist and turn, a chance to grow,
In the map of us, love's currents flow.

With every choice, a road unfolds,
In laughter's echo, life retold.
In shared adventures, dreams take flight,
In every moment, pure delight.

Through valleys deep and mountains high,
We navigate, you and I.
In every challenge, hand in hand,
Together bright, we take a stand.

The compass spins, our hearts align,
In unity, our souls entwine.
Through storms and sunshine, we will rise,
In the map of us, love never dies.

From every journey, lessons learned,
The flames of passion, brightly burned.
In every heartbeat, trust will guide,
The map of us, our love, our pride.

The Dance of Familiar Faces

In the twilight glow we meet,
Laughter echoing, soft and sweet.
Together in rhythms, hearts entwined,
Memories linger, our souls aligned.

Joy in movements, swift and free,
A circle of friends, harmony.
Each step a story, each glance a spark,
Illuminating shadows, lighting the dark.

With every twirl, we shed our fears,
Embracing moments, wiping tears.
A dance of spirit, a timeless song,
In this joyous gathering, we all belong.

We know the beats, like whispered sighs,
Familiar faces, familiar ties.
In our own rhythm, we find our place,
United forever, in the dance of grace.

As the stars above start to gleam,
We weave our tales, like a shared dream.
With open hearts and hands held tight,
We dance through shadows, into the light.

Silhouettes of Shared Dreams

In the quiet night, shadows play,
Silhouettes tell stories, drift away.
Under the moon's watchful gaze,
We share our hopes in a soft haze.

Voices whisper secrets, like the breeze,
In the stillness, we aim to please.
With every heartbeat, dreams take flight,
Carried on wings, into the night.

Hand in hand, we chase the stars,
Our dreams unbound, no hidden scars.
Together we rise, against the tide,
As kindred spirits, side by side.

Each silhouette, a reflection bright,
Crafting a future, igniting light.
In the canvas of dusk, we sketch our fate,
Brushing the world, as we create.

In the dawn's embrace, dreams align,
Fading into visions, so divine.
With every heartbeat, we become whole,
Silhouettes of dreams, writing our roll.

Colors of Comradeship

In vibrant hues, our stories blend,
A tapestry woven, with every friend.
Brushstrokes of laughter, splashes of tears,
Together we paint, through all the years.

Red of our passion, blue of the calm,
In every color, we find a balm.
Golden moments, shimmering bright,
Under the canvas of starry night.

With every shade, a tale unfolds,
In colors bold, we break the molds.
A palette of memories, rich and deep,
In comradeship's garden, our dreams we reap.

As seasons change, our colors shift,
Embracing the light, every tender gift.
Through every storm, through every fight,
Our comradeship shines, a guiding light.

In every sunset, we find our hue,
Colors of comradery, forever true.
With hearts united, we journey far,
In the gallery of life, we are the stars.

The Flow of Affection

In gentle waves, affection flows,
Carrying warmth wherever it goes.
With every heartbeat, a loving sound,
In the river of kindness, we are found.

Through sunlit valleys and whispered dreams,
We nurture hope, or so it seems.
With open arms, we welcome the day,
In the flow of love, we find our way.

Like streams converging, our paths entwine,
In the sacred waters, hearts combine.
Every drop a promise, pure and clear,
Reflecting the joy that we hold dear.

As tides may rise, and winds may change,
In the flow of affection, nothing feels strange.
With every ripple, we touch the deep,
Connecting our spirits, a bond to keep.

Through each ebb and flow, we stand tall,
In the journey of love, we're all called.
With hearts wide open, we gladly see,
The flow of affection will always be.

Windows into Our World

Through glass panes, we peek and see,
Life unfolds, wild and free.
Colors blend, shadows play,
Moments captured, day by day.

Whispers carried on the breeze,
Nature's dance among the trees.
Laughter echoes, hearts ignite,
Windows bright with pure delight.

In every frame, a story told,
Adventures captured, young and old.
Time may fade, yet we remain,
Witnessing joy, embracing pain.

Scenes of love, shadows of doubt,
Through the glass, we scream and shout.
Glimmers of dreams in every glow,
Windows offer a world to know.

So gaze upon that shifting light,
Each glance revealing morning bright.
Life's reflections, a timeless strand,
Windows into our heart's demand.

A Melody of Memories

In the air, a tune does sway,
Notes of laughter, come what may.
Softly sung, the tales unfold,
Melodies of memories, bright and bold.

Each refrain, a moment's grace,
Echoes linger in the space.
Whispers from the past unite,
Dancing softly in the night.

Harmonies of love and loss,
Through every gain, we bear the cross.
Strummed on strings of joy and pain,
Melody whispers in the rain.

Every chord, a heartbeat strong,
Together we write our song.
With each note, a life we weave,
In this symphony, we believe.

As time flows, let the music sing,
Reminding us of everything.
With every beat, we find our way,
In a melody of memories, we stay.

Glistening Moments

In twilight's glow, the world aglow,
Glistening moments in the flow.
Sunlit sparkles on the sea,
Whispers of what's meant to be.

Raindrops dance on leaves so green,
Creating magic, pure and clean.
Crystal clear and shining bright,
Moments treasured, pure delight.

Starlit skies above our gaze,
Radiant dreams in cosmic plays.
Fragments of time, so precious, rare,
Glistening moments everywhere.

With every heartbeat, life bestows,
Gifts of time, as nature flows.
In every breath, a chance to see,
The beauty in our jubilee.

So pause awhile, embrace the gleam,
In fleeting seconds, find the dream.
Capture joy in every glance,
Glistening moments, life's sweet dance.

Weaving through Time

Threads entangle, stories weave,
In every moment, we believe.
Patterns form, colors blend,
Tapestries of life extend.

Weaving memories, fierce and true,
Stitches of love in every view.
Through the loom of days gone by,
We craft our tales, we do not sigh.

Ancestral whispers guide our hand,
As we stitch together, bit by strand.
With hope and dreams, we intertwine,
Looms of fate, our stories shine.

In gentle threads, our past may flow,
Every color, a tale to show.
Weaving through time, together we stand,
United by history, heart in hand.

So let us gather, share our hearts,
In this fabric, each one part.
For every weave, a bond we make,
Through time we journey, awake.

Crescendo of Quiet Moments

In the hush of dawn's embrace,
Whispers weave through time and space.
Each tick of clocks, a tender sound,
In quiet corners, peace is found.

Sunlight spills on dewy grass,
Softly urging shadows to pass.
Nature hums a gentle tune,
As moments stretch beneath the moon.

In the stillness, hearts align,
Feeling sacred, pure, divine.
Breath by breath, we find our way,
In crescendo, night turns to day.

Laughter dances in the air,
Filling spaces, light and rare.
With every heartbeat, we compose,
A symphony where quiet grows.

Together in these sacred times,
We write our verses, share our rhymes.
In silence, love's sweet music plays,
A crescendo that softly stays.

Symphonies in Silence

In echoes of a distant thought,
The silence sings of battles fought.
Empty spaces hold their breath,
A symphony that conquers death.

Gentle winds through branches glide,
Nature's hush, a cherished guide.
Every rustle tells a tale,
In quiet hearts, true loves prevail.

Stars wink softly in the night,
Each twinkle whispers pure delight.
We find our rhythm in the dark,
With silence painting every spark.

A world unspoken, yet profound,
In harmony, we gather round.
With every pause, our souls connect,
In silent moments, we reflect.

Together, hand in hand we stand,
Creating music, life so grand.
Where silence reigns, our spirits rise,
In symphonies beneath the skies.

Caresses of Companionship

In gentle touch, we find our light,
A shared glance that feels just right.
Hands entwined in soft sunlight,
Companionship, our hearts ignite.

Whispers shared beneath the stars,
Filling dreams with love's avatars.
Every moment, joy unspoken,
In laughter's dance, our chains are broken.

Side by side, we face the day,
In shadows cast, our worries sway.
With every heartbeat, we compose,
A melody that sweetly flows.

Breath of life, in sync we breathe,
In every sigh, our hearts believe.
Caresses soft, the world feels bright,
In companionship, we take flight.

Together through this journey vast,
Letting go of fears amassed.
In each caress, we find a song,
With love as guide, we must be strong.

The Melody of Memory

In corridors of fleeting time,
Memories linger, softly chime.
Images dance like shadows cast,
In the present, we hold the past.

Each laugh, a note within our hearts,
A tapestry of life that starts.
Every echo tells a story,
In the silence, we find glory.

Sunlit days and starry nights,
Feelings wrapped in warm delights.
The melody of what once was,
Plays gently, just because.

In whispers of the leaves that fall,
Life's sweet echoes, we can recall.
In these moments, we still thrive,
With memories, our dreams derive.

Together, we shall weave and spin,
Every chapter holds a win.
In the dance of time, we sway,
The melody shall guide our way.

Tides of Togetherness

In the ebb and flow of time,
We find our hearts align,
With each wave that crashes,
We share a love divine.

By the shore, we dance and play,
As the sun rolls down,
Together, hand in hand,
For joy, we wear the crown.

Amidst the salty breeze,
Our whispers start to blend,
In this vast ocean,
You are my steadfast friend.

The stars steer our way,
In the deep of night,
Guiding us through shadows,
To each other's light.

Through every rise and fall,
Our bond will always sway,
In the tides of togetherness,
Forever we will stay.

Lighthouses of Loyalty

In the stormy seas of doubt,
You shine with steady grace,
A beacon in the night sky,
A warm and bright embrace.

When the world feels so cold,
And waves crash hard and fast,
Your light guides me onward,
A love that will not pass.

As the clouds gather round,
Your strength holds me true,
With every flicker, a promise,
I will always cherish you.

In the depths of turmoil,
Our hearts will never stray,
Like lighthouses standing tall,
We'll light the darkest way.

Together, we can weather
Each tempest's raging song,
With lighthouses of loyalty,
Our bond will ever strong.

The Essence of Entwined Paths

In the garden where we grow,
Our roots entwined below,
With every petal's grace,
We find a deeper flow.

We weave our dreams like threads,
In the fabric of the night,
With laughter guiding us,
We share our hearts' delight.

As we stroll through tangled woods,
With shadows soft and light,
Each step reflects a journey,
In the glimmer of the night.

The essence of our journey,
Like rivers bound to meet,
In every twist and turn,
We make our lives complete.

Through the seasons, we shall roam,
Entwined in love's sweet path,
Together, forevermore,
In joy and shared heart's laugh.

The Beauty in Shared Breath

In the quiet of the night,
Our breaths create a song,
A rhythm soft and tender,
Binding us where we belong.

With every sigh and whisper,
We dance in harmony,
In the space between our words,
Is where our souls run free.

The beauty in shared moments,
In the gaze of your sweet eyes,
Reflecting all our secrets,
Underneath the starlit skies.

Through laughter and through sorrows,
Together we shall tread,
In the beauty of our union,
In every word we've said.

As the dawn brings light anew,
We'll face what lies ahead,
In the beauty of shared breath,
Our love will gently spread.

Fables of Interconnection

In the forest whispers, trees entwine,
Roots beneath, a hidden line.
Birds in chorus, a tune so sweet,
Nature's story, a dance of feet.

Streams of silver, merging flows,
Reflecting light, where harmony grows.
Each creature knows their part to play,
In this fable, night meets day.

From mountains high to valleys low,
Connections bloom, like seeds we sow.
Voices mingle with the breeze,
In the silence, hearts find ease.

Each star above has its tale spun,
Linked by fate, they glow as one.
With every whisper, bonds grow tight,
In Interconnection, we find our light.

Starlit Conversations

Underneath the vast night sky,
Thoughts take flight, as wishes fly.
Stars are scribes of dreams untold,
In their shimmer, secrets unfold.

Wisps of cloud drift softly by,
In the quiet, spirits sigh.
Every twinkle, a voice so clear,
Bridging gaps, we hold them dear.

Moonlight dances on gentle waves,
Guiding lost souls, brave and brave.
In the stillness, we find our peace,
In starlit chats, our worries cease.

Echoes linger on the breeze,
Murmured hopes, like rustling leaves.
Conversations deep and bright,
In the cosmos, hearts ignite.

The Fusion of Spirits

Fire and water, a clash so bold,
In their embrace, new stories unfold.
Breath of earth, song of the sky,
Together they dance, a love's reply.

Crimson dreams and azure streams,
In the night, we weave our themes.
Echoes of laughter, shadows of grace,
In fusion of spirits, we find our place.

Whispers of winds, a guiding thread,
In every heartbeat, life is fed.
Elements merge, as souls ignite,
To create a world, radiant and bright.

In this tapestry, bold and free,
Together we weave, you and me.
From every clash, new forms arise,
In the fusion, our hearts harmonize.

Portraits by Candlelight

In the glow of soft candlelight,
Faces emerge from the quiet night.
Stories painted in shadows' embrace,
Every flicker reveals a trace.

Profiles dance on the old brick wall,
Whispers echo, as shadows call.
In laughter shared and secrets told,
Timeless moments, a warmth to hold.

Every heartbeat, a brushstroke fine,
Capturing laughter, fears entwined.
In the still, time takes its flight,
Portraits lived in candlelight.

As embers fade, the tales remain,
In dreams, we stroll the lanes again.
With every candle softly burned,
A life's canvas, lovingly turned.

Chords of Intertwined Lives

In shadows we dance, two souls align,
With every heartbeat, our fates entwine.
Through trials we weather, through laughter we soar,
In the tapestry woven, we gather and more.

Like a melody played on a gentle breeze,
Your laughter lingers, my spirit it frees.
With threads of connection, so vibrant and bright,
We illuminate darkness, we spark up the night.

In moments of silence, our hearts interlace,
A symphony born from this sacred space.
With every note sung, with every tear shed,
We find in each other the words left unsaid.

The rhythm of life in this dance we share,
Two wandering souls bound by love and care.
As seasons change colors, we stand side by side,
In chords of forever, in hope, we abide.

Whispers in the Wind

The wind carries tales, soft as a sigh,
Of dreams left unspoken, of wishes that fly.
In the hush of the evening, secrets unwind,
In whispers of nature, our hearts are entwined.

We chase after echoes beneath the moonlight,
As shadows dance gracefully, lost from our sight.
Each flutter of leaves tells a story anew,
In the silence surrounding, I search just for you.

From mountains to valleys, the whispers emerge,
In every sweet breeze, our spirits converge.
With each gust that blows, my heart skips a beat,
In this vast universe, our souls gently meet.

The night wraps around us, a delicate veil,
With stars as our compass, we set forth to sail.
In whispers of wonder, the world comes alive,
In the arms of the wind, we learn how to thrive.

The Harmony of Us

In the quiet of morning, our voices unite,
Like birdsong at dawn, bringing warmth to the light.
With each gentle note, our hopes intertwine,
Creating a symphony, a love so divine.

Through valleys of sorrow, through peaks that inspire,
We fuel the flames of our heart's true desire.
In the dance of the seasons, we sway side by side,
In the harmony found, in the love that won't hide.

With laughter as rhythm and trust as the beat,
We compose a melody that's soothing, yet sweet.
No matter the trials the world may insist,
In the harmony of us, it's hope that won't twist.

Together we flourish like vines in the sun,
In the garden of life, our journeys begun.
With each note we carry, together we grow,
In the harmony of us, our spirits will glow.

Mirrors of Understanding

In the depths of your eyes, I see my own soul,
Reflected in silence, each piece makes me whole.
With whispers of kindness and gestures so true,
We weave through the fabric, just me and you.

In shared moments sacred, a truth starts to bloom,
Like flowers in spring, banishing gloom.
Through trials and triumphs, our paths intertwine,
In mirrors of understanding, your heart beats with mine.

With empathy's touch, we unravel the night,
Lifting each other, embracing the light.
In the language of love, we find our sweet pace,
In mirrors of understanding, there's grace in our space.

So here's to the journey, the roads we have tread,
In every shared heartbeat, in words left unsaid.
For in the reflections of life we create,
We learn to be patient, we learn to be great.